asian selfie

selfie

/ˈsɛlfi/

Saznajte kako izgovarati

noun

INFORMAL

noun: **selfie**; plural noun: **selfies**; noun: **selfy**

1. a photograph that one has taken of oneself, typically one taken with a smartphone or webcam and shared via social media.

"occasional selfies are acceptable, but posting a new picture of yourself every day isn't necessary"

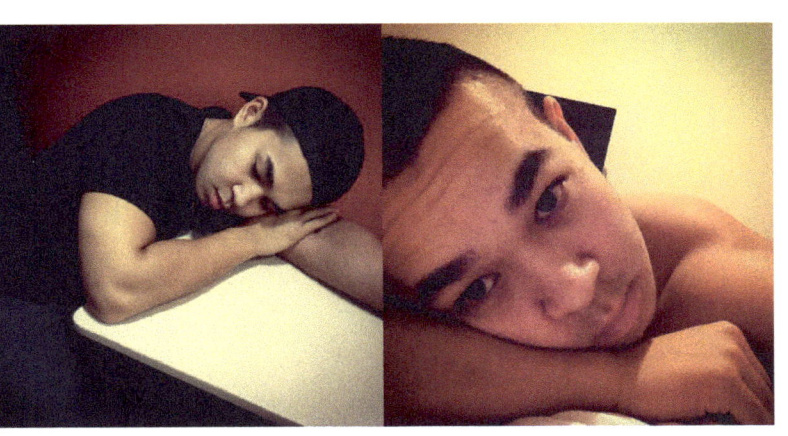

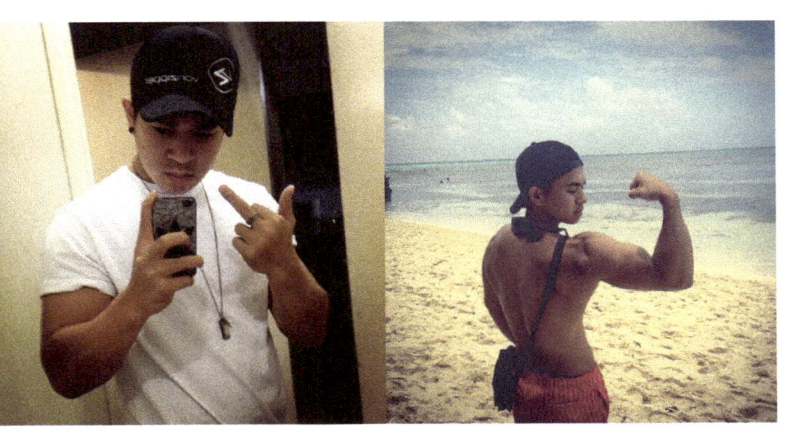

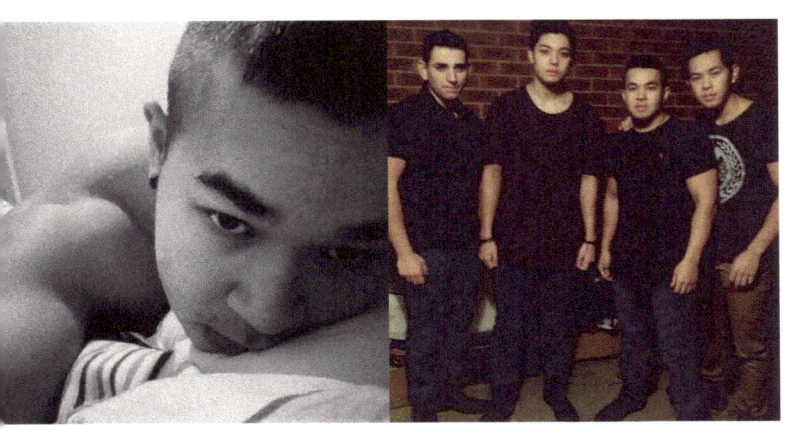

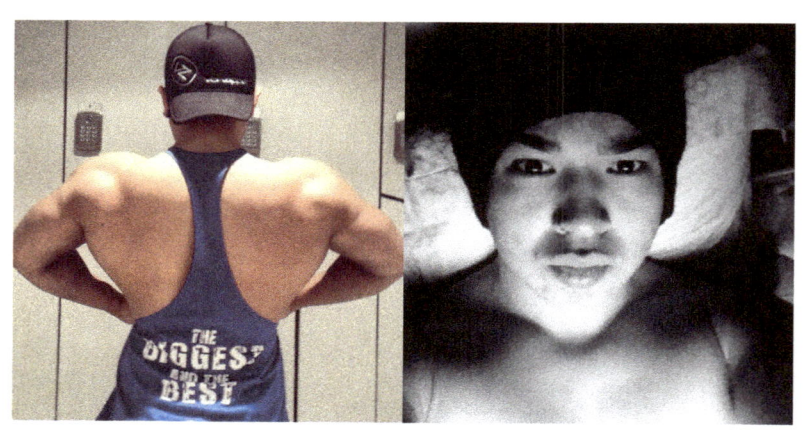

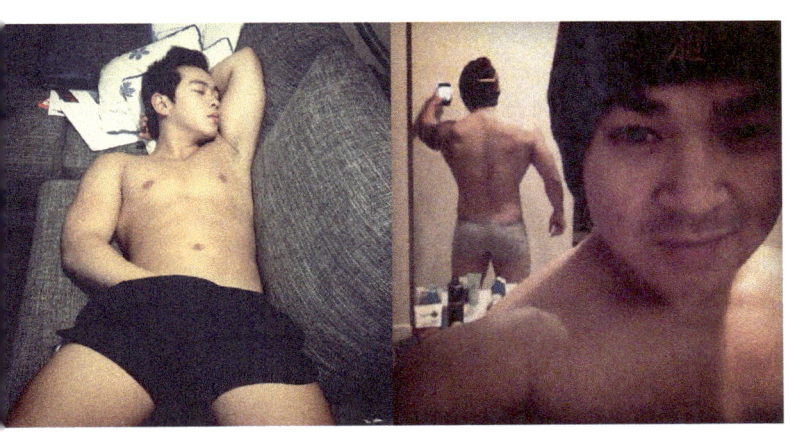

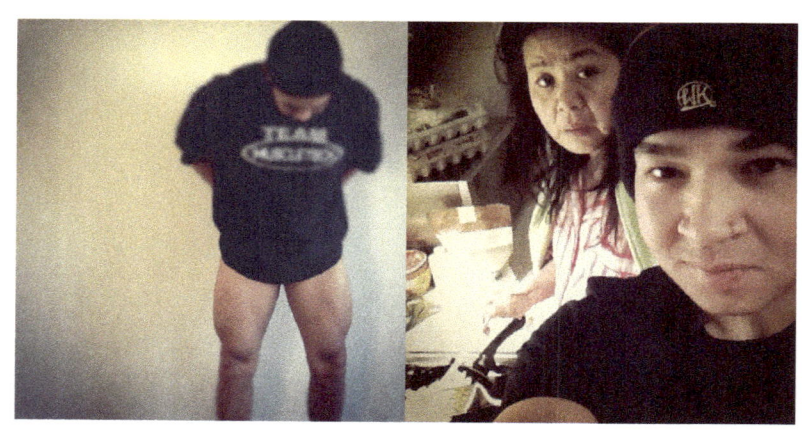

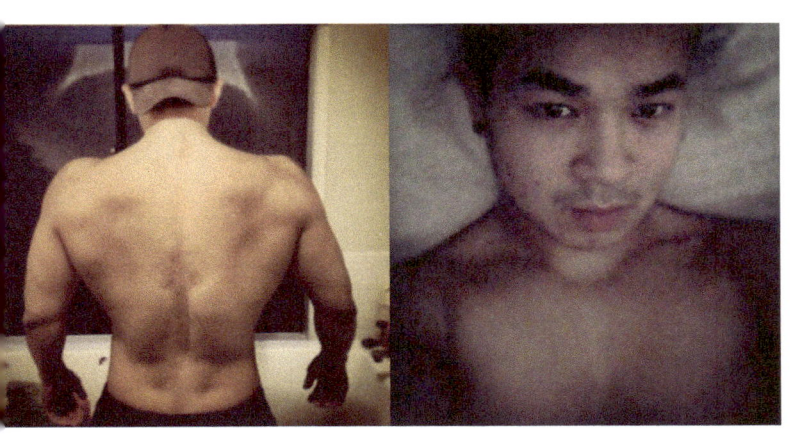

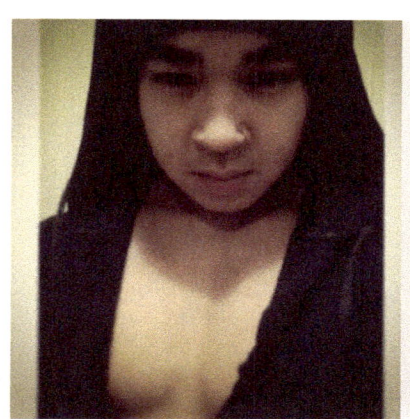
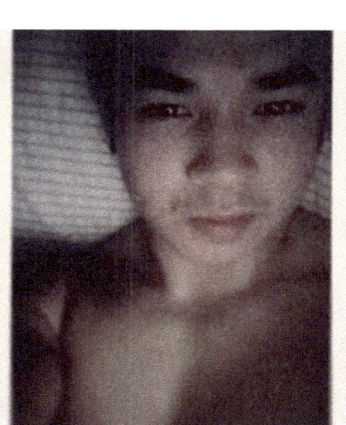

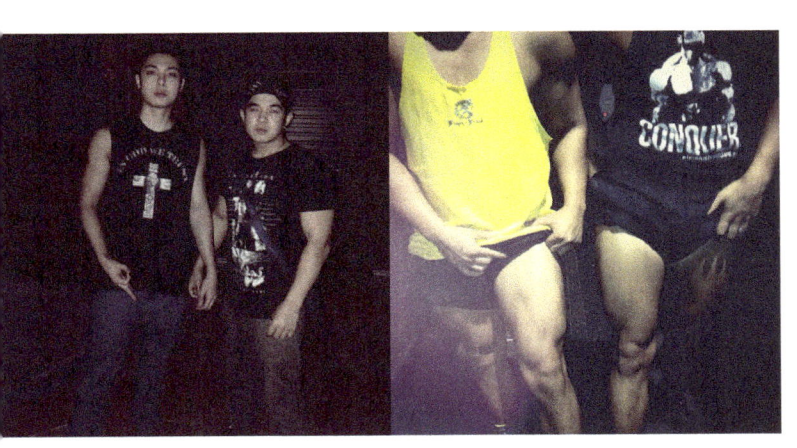

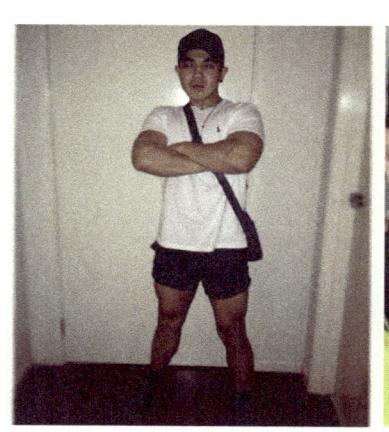

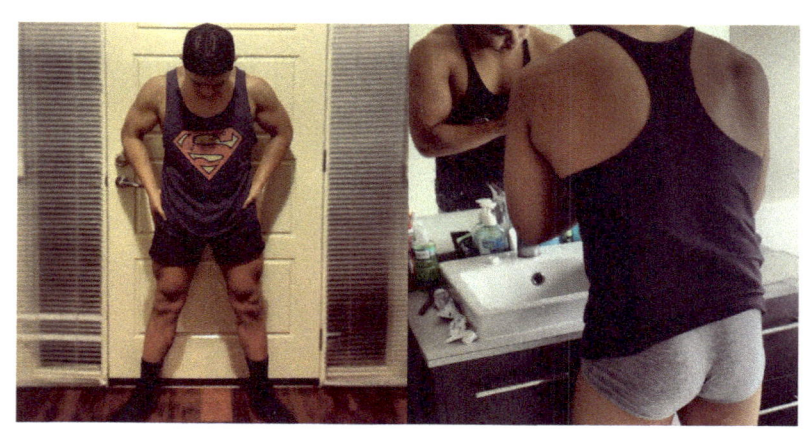

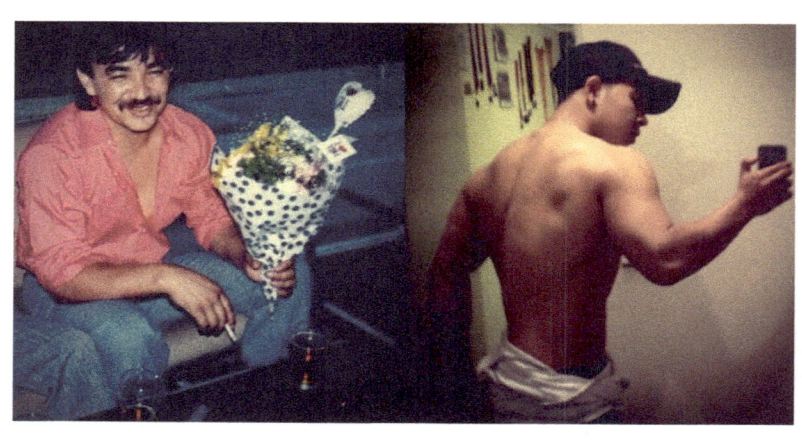

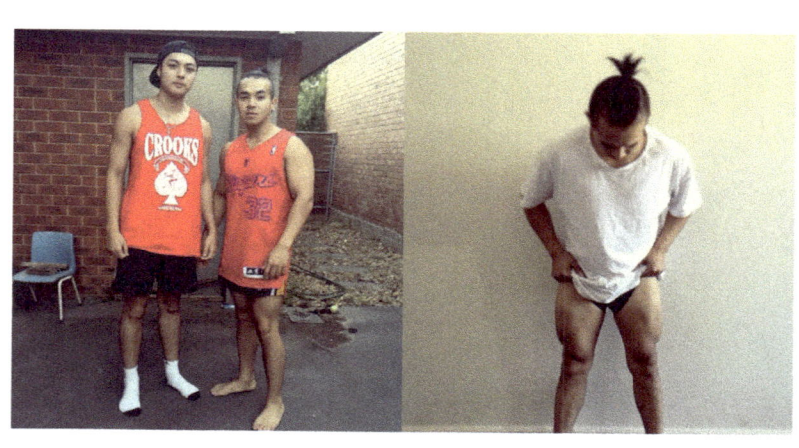

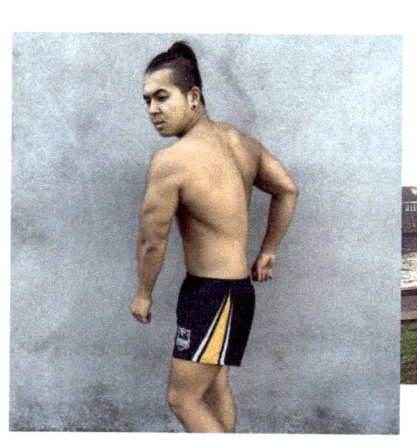

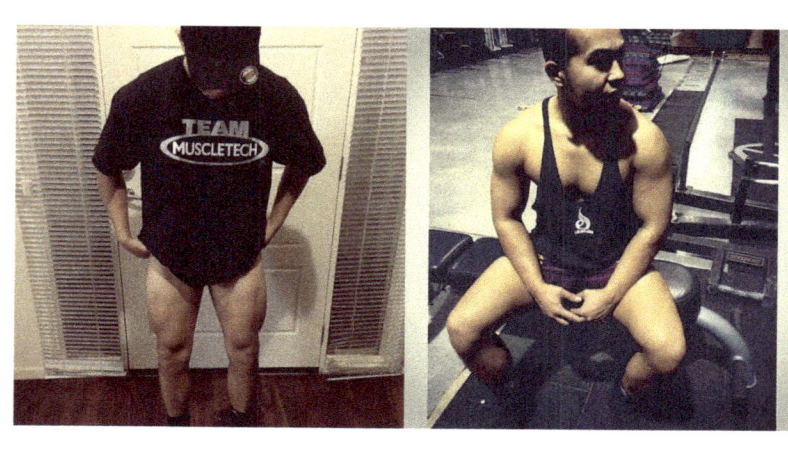

CPSIA information can be obtained
at www.ICGtesting.com
Printed in the USA
BVHW022011280719
554531BV00011B/397/P

9 780464 086864